CW00401991

Vegetables

MARY CADOGAN

MEREHURST
LONDON

Contents

Managing Editor: Janet Illsley
Photographer: James Murphy
Designer: Sue Storey
Food Stylists: Mary Cadogan and Annie Aitken
Photographic Stylist: Maria Jacques
Typeset by Angel Graphics
Colour separation by Fotographics, UK - Hong Kong
Printed in Italy by New Interlitho S.p.A.

Published 1991 by Merehurst Ltd,
Ferry House, 51/57 Lacy Road, Putney, London SW15 1PR

ISBN: 1 85391 142 9 (Cased)
ISBN: 1 85391 230 1 (Paperback)

A catalogue record for this book is available from the British Library

NOTES

All spoon measures are level: 1 tablespoon = 15ml spoon; 1 teaspoon = 5ml spoon.
Use fresh herbs and freshly ground black pepper unless otherwise stated.

Introduction

It was not so long ago that vegetables were a mere after-thought to a meal. Meat or fish took centre stage and vegetables were simply boiled and offered up as a filler. How things have changed, as we have come to realise that vegetables can add infinite variety to our meals.

I grow many of my own vegetables and get immense satisfaction from seeing healthy shoots emerging from the soil or finding that the first young beans have formed among the foliage. There is so much to celebrate with every season: the arrival of summer and the first plate of tender asparagus with herbed butter sauce; or rushing home to pod your first basket of peas. As the year moves on and the nights turn chilly, a dish of baked cabbage with fennel, or cauliflower studded with spices, has a different attraction.

Of course many of our vegetables are brought in from other countries, so the seasons become blurred. This isn't a bad thing, as when we tire of endless winter root vegetables, for example, we can revive our jaded appetites with some okra, baby corn, or Chinese greens, perhaps.

I am not a vegetarian, but while devising, testing and tasting these recipes – mainly as accompaniments – I found that serving maybe three or four of them together made an exciting meal and meat became an irrelevance. A winter meal might include leeks with wine and mustard, carrot and celeriac bake and potato skins with garlic sauce. For a lighter summer menu try stuffed courgettes (zucchini), crispy new potatoes and spinach with pine nuts. The vegetable mixtures at the end of the book need little more than a salad and bread to make them complete.

Writing this book has given me particular pleasure, which I hope I can pass on to you as you try the recipes.

Mary Cadogan

Asparagus with Herb Sauce

Serve this tasty dish on its own as a starter or light lunch to really appreciate the rich tangy sauce.

750g (1½ lb) asparagus
salt and pepper to taste
HERB VINEGAR SAUCE:
2 egg yolks
2 tablespoons tarragon vinegar
125g (4oz) unsalted butter
1 tablespoon chopped mixed herbs, ie tarragon, chives and parsley

1 Break off and discard the tough woody ends from the asparagus. Peel the ends of the stalks. Place the asparagus in a steaming basket over a large saucepan of boiling water and sprinkle with salt. Cover and cook for about 10 minutes, until tender.
2 Meanwhile make the sauce. Place the egg yolks and vinegar in a small heatproof bowl over a pan of barely simmering water. Whisk together until slightly thickened, taking care that the bowl does not become too hot otherwise the sauce could curdle.
3 Whisking the sauce constantly, add the butter a small piece at a time, allowing each piece to be absorbed before adding the next. When all the butter has been added, the sauce should be thick and smooth. Remove from the heat and add the herbs, salt and pepper.
4 Arrange the asparagus on 4 warmed individual plates. Pour a little sauce over the centre of the stalks and serve immediately. *Serves 4.*

BROCCOLI WITH HERB VINEGAR SAUCE: Divide 500g (1lb) broccoli into florets and steam or cook in boiling salted water for 7-10 minutes, until just tender. Spoon over the herb vinegar sauce and serve as a delicious accompaniment to grilled meat or fish.

Broad Beans with Dill

Fresh young broad beans are an early summer treat. Avoid pods where the beans are almost bursting out, as their flavour will be inferior. Serve this accompaniment hot, or cold as a salad.

1.5kg (3lb) broad beans
1 tablespoon olive oil
1 onion, thinly sliced
1 clove garlic, crushed
125ml (4 fl oz/½ cup) water
1 tablespoon chopped dill
½ teaspoon sugar
salt and pepper to taste

1 Remove the broad beans from their pods. Heat the oil in a saucepan, add the onion and fry gently for about 5 minutes, until softened and lightly browned. Add the garlic and broad beans and stir well. Cook for 1 minute.
2 Add the water and bring to the boil. Lower the heat, cover and cook for 12-15 minutes, until the beans are tender. Add the dill, sugar, salt and pepper and cook for a further 1 minute. Serve hot or cold. *Serves 4-6.*

Asparagus with Waterchestnuts

The slightly cheaper, thin sprue asparagus is ideal for this dish.

250g (8oz) thin asparagus
230g (7oz) can waterchestnuts
2 tablespoons sunflower oil
1 teaspoon grated fresh root (green) ginger
3 tablespoons finely chopped spring onions (green shallots)
1 tablespoon soy sauce
1-2 tablespoons water
salt and pepper to taste

1 Cut the asparagus diagonally into 2.5cm (1 inch) lengths. Drain the waterchestnuts and slice them thinly.
2 Heat the oil in a wok or frying pan with a lid. Add the ginger and spring onions (shallots) and fry for 1 minute. Add the asparagus and waterchestnuts and stir well. Add the soy sauce, water, salt and pepper and bring to the boil. Lower the heat, cover and cook for 6-8 minutes, until the asparagus is tender. Serve immediately. *Serves 4-6.*

Peas with Sorrel

Fresh peas taste so different from frozen ones that they could be another vegetable. It's worth shelling all those peas for this dish.

1kg (2lb) fresh peas in pods
125g (4oz) sorrel leaves
30g (1oz) butter
salt and pepper to taste
2 spring onions (green shallots), chopped
2 tablespoons single (light) cream

1 Shell the peas and place in a pan with the sorrel and butter. Heat gently until the butter is bubbling, then add sufficient boiling water to just cover the peas. Cover and cook gently for 10-15 minutes, until the peas are almost tender.
2 Remove the lid and boil steadily for 2-3 minutes to reduce the liquid. Lower the heat and stir in the salt, pepper, spring onions (shallots) and cream. Warm through gently and serve immediately. *Serves 4-6.*

Broad Beans with Peppercorns

1.5kg (3lb) broad beans
few marjoram sprigs
few thyme sprigs
1 teaspoon green peppercorns
30g (1oz) butter
2 teaspoons plain flour
125ml (4 fl oz/½ cup) dry white wine
salt and pepper to taste

1 Pod the broad beans and place in a pan with the herbs and enough water to just cover. Bring to the boil, then lower the heat, cover and cook for about 10 minutes until just tender. Drain, reserving the cooking liquor.
2 Meanwhile coarsely crush the peppercorns and mix into the butter. Melt the butter in a saucepan, add the flour and cook for 1 minute. Stir in the wine and cook, stirring, until thickened and smooth. Add 4-5 tablespoons of the reserved liquor, stirring until the sauce just coats the back of the spoon. Season well, then add the broad beans. Heat through gently before serving. *Serves 6-8.*

Stuffed Courgettes (Zucchini)

Of course you can use the more familiar long courgettes (zucchini) for this recipe, but round ones are easier to stuff and they look splendid. Some supermarkets now stock them in the summer, or you can always try growing your own.

125g (4oz/2/3 cup) bulgar wheat
4 round courgettes (zucchini), about 125g (4oz) each
30g (1oz) butter
1 small onion, finely chopped
1 clove garlic, crushed
30g (1oz/1/4 cup) chopped almonds
handful of mint leaves, chopped
2 tablespoons chopped parsley
2 tablespoons lemon juice
2 tablespoons natural yogurt
salt and pepper to taste
60g (2oz) Cheddar cheese, grated

1 Preheat the oven to 190C (375F/Gas 5). Place the bulgar wheat in a bowl, pour over sufficient boiling water to cover and leave for 5 minutes, until the grains are swollen; drain well.
2 Cut the tops off the courgettes (zucchini); set aside. Scoop out the flesh, leaving 2cm (3/4 inch) shells, and chop finely.
3 Melt the butter in a saucepan. Add the onion, garlic and almonds and fry, stirring, until golden brown. Add the courgette (zucchini) flesh and fry for 2-3 minutes, until softened. Add the bulgar wheat, mint, parsley, lemon juice, yogurt, salt and pepper and stir well to mix.
4 Pile the stuffing into the courgette (zucchini) shells and stand upright in a buttered roasting tin or ovenproof dish in which they fit snugly. Sprinkle with cheese and replace the tops. Bake in the preheated oven for 30-35 minutes, until the courgettes (zucchini) are tender and the filling is golden brown.
5 Serve as a starter or as an accompaniment to roasts and simple meat dishes. *Serves 4 or 8.*

NOTE: If using long courgettes (zucchini), cut them in half lengthwise, scoop out the flesh and fill both halves.

Grilled Mustard Tomatoes

Use large ripe tomatoes which have a full sweet flavour to offset the sharp mustard in this piquant dressing.

4-6 large tomatoes
DRESSING:
1 tablespoon olive oil
1 tablespoon lemon juice
1 teaspoon clear honey
1 teaspoon wholegrain mustard
salt to taste
TO GARNISH:
chopped parsley

1 Preheat the grill to medium. Cut the tomatoes in half and place on the grill rack.
2 Mix together the dressing ingredients in a small bowl and brush over the tomatoes. Grill for about 5 minutes, basting occasionally. Sprinkle with chopped parsley and serve hot. *Serves 4.*

Green Beans with Dijon Mustard

500g (1lb) French beans
salt to taste
30g (1oz) butter
1 tablespoon chopped parsley
2 spring onions (green shallots), chopped
2-3 teaspoons Dijon mustard

1 Top and tail the beans, then steam or cook in boiling water to cover for 5-10 minutes, until just tender. Drain if necessary, then sprinkle lightly with salt.
2 Melt the butter in a saucepan, add the parsley and spring onions (shallots) and fry gently for 1 minute. Stir in the mustard and 1 tablespoon water. Add the beans, turn to coat with the sauce and heat through. Serve hot with baked fish or chicken. *Serves 4-6.*

VARIATION: Runner beans can also be cooked in this way. Top tail, and string them, then slice before cooking.

Beans with Garlic & Tomato

This is my favourite way of serving French beans – its simple yet totally delicious. We often eat this as a meal in itself, with nothing more than some crusty bread to mop up the juices.

500g (1lb) French beans
2 ripe tomatoes
salt and pepper to taste
3 tablespoons olive oil
1 clove garlic, finely chopped

1 Top and tail the French beans, then rinse and drain. Skin the tomatoes and chop roughly. Cook the beans in boiling salted water to cover for 7-10 minutes, until just tender; drain well.
2 Heat the oil in a saucepan, add the garlic and tomatoes and cook gently for about 5 minutes. Add the French beans and stir well. Season with pepper, and salt if necessary. Cover and cook gently for 2-3 minutes. Serve hot or cold. *Serves 4.*

NOTE: To skin tomatoes, spear on a fork and hold over a gas flame for 15-30 seconds, turning until the skin blisters, then peel away the skins. Alternatively plunge the tomatoes into a bowl of boiling hot water and leave for 30 seconds, then peel.

COURGETTES (ZUCCHINI) WITH GARLIC AND TOMATO: Replace the French beans with courgettes (zucchini). Cut into slices and steam or cook in boiling water until barely tender before adding to the tomato.

Spinach with Pine Nuts

A tasty accompaniment to serve hot with kebabs, grilled meat or fish. It can also be served cold as a salad – refresh the spinach in cold running water immediately after cooking and stir in a little extra yogurt.

1kg (2lb) spinach leaves
salt and pepper to taste
freshly grated nutmeg
1 tablespoon sunflower oil
1 clove garlic, finely chopped
2 tablespoons pine nuts
2 tablespoons raisins
2 tablespoons thick Greek yogurt

1 Wash the spinach in several changes of cold water, picking out any discoloured leaves. Place the spinach in a saucepan with just the water clinging to the leaves after washing. Season with salt, pepper and nutmeg to taste and heat gently until the spinach leaves start to wilt. Shake the pan, cover and cook gently for 3-5 minutes until the spinach is tender.
2 Drain the spinach in a colander, pressing out as much liquid as possible. Chop the leaves using the edge of a saucer.
3 Heat the oil in a frying pan. Add the garlic, pine nuts and raisins and fry gently for about 2 minutes until the pine nuts are pale golden. Add the spinach, stir well and heat through. Stir in the yogurt, then taste and add more seasoning if necessary. Serve immediately. *Serves 4-6.*

Cucumber with Red Pepper

Cooked cucumber is quite a revelation and, combined with red pepper, makes an attractive dish to serve with fish and chicken.

1 cucumber
½ red pepper, seeded
30g (1oz) butter
salt and pepper to taste

1 Peel the cucumber and cut into 4 or 5 equal pieces, then cut each piece into matchsticks. Place in a colander and sprinkle lightly with salt. Leave to drain over a bowl.
2 Preheat the grill to high. Cut the pepper in half and grill, skin side up, until charred. When cool enough to handle, peel off the skin and slice thinly.
3 Rinse the cucumber and pat dry with absorbent kitchen paper. Heat the butter in a saucepan until foaming. Add the cucumber and stir until evenly coated with butter, then cover and cook gently for about 5 minutes, until just tender. Add the pepper and stir well. Heat through, taste and add pepper, and salt if necessary. *Serves 4.*

Marrow with Oyster Sauce

1 medium marrow
1 tablespoon sunflower oil
1 clove garlic
1 teaspoon grated fresh root (green) ginger
3 tablespoons oyster sauce
3 tablespoons water
salt to taste
2 tablespoons chopped spring onions (green shallots)

1 Peel the marrow, halve lengthwise and scoop out the seeds. Chop the flesh into 2.5cm (1 inch) cubes.
2 Heat the oil in a saucepan, add the garlic and ginger and fry for 1 minute, until lightly browned. Add the marrow and stir well. Add the oyster sauce and water and bring to the boil. Cover and simmer for 5-8 minutes, until the marrow is tender but not too soft. Taste and add salt if necessary.
3 Serve sprinkled with spring onion (shallot). *Serves 4-6.*

Baby Beets with Chive Butter

This is a good way of using those bunches of small fresh beetroot that appear in the shops early in the summer.

500g (1lb) baby beets
30g (1oz) butter
grated rind of 1 lemon
1 tablespoon lemon juice
salt and pepper to taste
1 tablespoon snipped chives

1 Trim the leaves from the beets, leaving about 2.5cm (1 inch) attached, taking care not to split the beet skins. Wash thoroughly and place in a saucepan with water to cover. Bring to the boil, then cook for 1½-2 hours; drain. When cool enough to handle, rub off the skins.
2 Mash the butter with the lemon rind. Place in a saucepan and heat gently. Add the beets and cook, stirring, for 5 minutes. Sprinkle with lemon juice, salt, pepper and chives and cook for 2 minutes. Serve hot. *Serves 4-6.*

Glazed Baby Turnips

Use small sweet turnips and only peel if the skins are tough. These are delicious served with duck or pork.

500g (1lb) baby turnips
2 teaspoons sugar
60g (2oz) butter
salt and pepper to taste
125ml (4 fl oz/½ cup) water

1 Trim the turnips, leaving a little tuft of stalk on each. Peel or scrub them, then place in a small saucepan with the sugar, butter, salt, pepper and water. Bring to the boil, then cover and cook gently for 10-12 minutes, until the turnips are just tender.
2 Remove the lid and boil hard to reduce the liquid to a glaze. Serve hot. *Serves 4.*

Crusty Potatoes with Gruyère

Bake these delicious new potatoes in a shallow dish to ensure they all get their fair share of the crust.

750g (1½lb) even-sized new potatoes
salt and pepper to taste
60g (2oz) butter, melted
60g (2oz) gruyère cheese, grated
60g (2oz/½ cup) dried breadcrumbs
1 tablespoon snipped chives
1 tablespoon finely chopped rosemary

1 Preheat the oven to 190C (375F/Gas 5). Scrub the potatoes, then parboil in salted water for about 15 minutes. Drain and place in a shallow ovenproof dish. Pour over half the butter, season and toss the potatoes until evenly coated.
2 Mix together the cheese, breadcrumbs, herbs, salt and pepper. Sprinkle evenly over the potatoes, then drizzle the remaining butter over the top.
3 Bake for 30 minutes, or until the topping is crisp and golden brown and the potatoes are cooked. *Serves 4.*

Crispy New Potatoes

New potatoes cooked this way become crispy on the outside and soft and melting on the inside. They are irresistible.

500g-750g (1-1½lb) small new potatoes
2 tablespoons olive oil
1 teaspoon paprika
1 teaspoon dried oregano
2 tablespoons finely chopped spring onion (green shallot)
salt and pepper to taste

1 Preheat the oven to 200C (400F/Gas 6). Scrub the potatoes, dry well and place in a roasting tin. In a small bowl, mix together the oil, paprika, oregano, spring onion (shallot), salt and pepper. Pour over the potatoes and turn until evenly coated.
2 Bake in the oven for 45-55 minutes, until tender, stirring once or twice during cooking. Serve hot. *Serves 4-6.*

Leeks with Wine & Mustard

This dish is finished off under the grill, but if you prefer to prepare it up to that point well in advance, pop it into a moderately hot oven for about 20 minutes before serving instead.

750g (1½lb) leeks
1 bouquet garni
2 cloves
15g (½oz) butter
125ml (4 fl oz/½ cup) vegetable stock
5 tablespoons dry white wine
salt and pepper to taste
1 tablespoon French mustard
3 tablespoons dried brown breadcrumbs

1 Wash the leeks thoroughly and cut into 4cm (1½ inch) lengths. Place in a saucepan with the bouquet garni, cloves, butter, stock, wine, salt and pepper. Bring to the boil, cover and cook for 12-15 minutes, until the leeks are just tender. Drain the leeks, reserving the cooking liquid.
2 Strain the cooking liquid back into the pan, then boil rapidly to reduce by half. Arrange the drained leeks in a buttered shallow ovenproof dish. Add the mustard to the reduced cooking juices, stir well and pour over the leeks.
3 Preheat the grill to moderately hot. Sprinkle the breadcrumbs over the leeks and grill until the topping is crisp and golden brown. Serve hot. *Serves 4-6.*

VARIATION: To serve as a cold side dish, replace the butter with 1 tablespoon olive oil and omit the topping. Allow the cooking liquid to cool before adding the mustard, together with 2 tablespoons thick Greek yogurt. Add to the leeks and toss to coat evenly.

Cauliflower with Tomato

When flavoursome tomatoes are available, use 3 or 4 skinned and chopped ones in place of the canned tomatoes.

1 cauliflower
1 tablespoon oil
250g (8oz) canned chopped tomatoes
1 tablespoon chopped celery leaves
1 tablespoon tomato purée (paste)
3 spring onions (green shallots), chopped
salt and pepper to taste
2 tablespoons chopped parsley

1 Cut the cauliflower into florets and cook in boiling salted water until just tender, about 10 minutes. Drain and immediately refresh under cold running water to stop further cooking.
2 Place the oil, tomatoes, celery leaves, tomato purée (paste), spring onions (shallots) and seasoning in a saucepan. Bring to the boil, then simmer for about 5 minutes, until pulpy. Add the cauliflower and stir well. Cover and cook for a further 5 minutes. Serve immediately, sprinkled with parsley. *Serves 4-6.*

Sweet & Soy Leeks

750g (1½ lb) leeks
2 tablespoons water
2 tablespoons plum jam
2 tablespoons soy sauce

1 Trim the leeks, then cut them in half lengthwise. Wash thoroughly, halve lengthwise again, then cut into 5cm (2 inch) lengths. Place in a saucepan with the water and cook, covered, for about 5 minutes, until slightly softened but still crunchy. Drain if necessary.
2 In the same saucepan, heat together the jam and soy sauce, stirring all the time until the jam has dissolved. Add the leeks and heat through for about 2 minutes. Serve hot. *Serves 4.*

Colcannon

Serve this traditional Irish dish with boiled or baked ham. This is comfort food at its best!

500g (1lb) cabbage
500g (1lb) potatoes
6 large spring onions (green shallots), finely chopped
125ml (4 fl oz/½ cup) milk
freshly grated nutmeg
salt and pepper to taste
60g (2oz) butter, melted
shredded spring onion (green shallot) to garnish

1 Finely shred the cabbage, then steam or cook in boiling water to cover for 12-15 minutes, until tender. Peel the potatoes, cut into chunks and cook in boiling salted water until tender; drain and mash. Meanwhile simmer the spring onions (shallots) in the milk, with nutmeg to taste, for 5 minutes.

2 Mash the cabbage into the potatoes, then gradually mash in the milk with flavourings, salt, pepper and butter. Reheat gently if necessary. Serve piping hot, topped with shredded spring onion (shallot). *Serves 4-6.*

Mustard & Coriander Cauliflower

1 cauliflower
2 tablespoons oil
2 teaspoons black mustard seeds
2 tablespoons chopped coriander leaves
4 tablespoons water
salt and pepper to taste

1 Cut the cauliflower into florets. Heat the oil in a wok or frying pan with a lid, add the mustard seeds and fry until they start to pop. Add the cauliflower and stir until evenly coated with mustard seeds. Cook, stirring for about 10 minutes.

2 Add the remaining ingredients and stir well. Cover and cook for 10-15 minutes, until the cauliflower is tender, but retains some crunch. Serve hot. *Serves 4-6.*

Baked Cabbage with Fennel

The aniseed flavour of fennel complements cabbage particularly well. You can assemble this dish several hours in advance, ready to pop it into the oven when needed.

500g (1lb) cabbage
250g (8oz) fennel bulb
1 onion
2 tablespoons olive oil
2 eggs
185ml (6 fl oz/¾ cup) milk
salt and pepper to taste
2 tablespoons dried breadcrumbs
2 tablespoons grated Parmesan cheese

1 Shred the cabbage finely, discarding the core. Quarter the fennel bulb, cut away the root and thinly slice the bulb. Chop the fennel leaves. Thinly slice the onion.
2 Heat the oil in a saucepan. Add the onion and fry gently for about 5 minutes until softened. Add the cabbage, fennel bulb and leaves. Season with salt and pepper and stir well. Cover and cook gently, stirring occasionally, for about 15 minutes. Transfer to a greased ovenproof pie dish or gratin dish.
3 Preheat the oven to 160C (325F/Gas 3). Beat together the eggs, milk, salt and pepper. Pour evenly over the cabbage mixture. Mix together the breadcrumbs and cheese and sprinkle evenly over the top.
4 Bake in the oven for 45 minutes, until the egg mixture has set and the topping is golden brown. Serve hot on its own as a warming supper dish, or as a tasty accompaniment to roast or grilled meats. *Serves 4-6.*

VARIATION: For a more substantial supper dish, fry 4-6 rashers chopped back bacon with the onion.

Glazed Winter Radish

Winter radishes come in various shapes and sizes and taste quite similar to turnip. Indeed, when they are unavailable, you can use turnips instead.

60g (2oz) butter
4 shallots, chopped
500g (1lb) winter radish, peeled and chopped
2 tablespoons wine vinegar
125ml (4 fl oz/½ cup) water
salt and pepper to taste
chopped parsley to garnish

1 Melt the butter in a small saucepan, add the shallots and cook gently for 4-5 minutes until softened. Add the radish and fry gently for about 5 minutes, until lightly coloured. Add the vinegar, water, salt and pepper and bring to the boil.
2 Cover and simmer for 15-20 minutes, until the radish is tender. If there is too much liquid, uncover and boil rapidly for a few minutes to reduce. Serve hot, sprinkled with parsley. *Serves 4-6.*

Puffed Parsnip

500g (1lb) parsnips
salt and pepper to taste
60g (2oz) butter
3 tablespoons cream
¼ teaspoon grated nutmeg
1 egg, beaten
2 tablespoons breadcrumbs

1 Peel and halve the parsnips, discard any woody cores and cut into chunks. Cook in boiling salted water for 15-20 minutes, until tender. Drain well.
2 Preheat the oven to 180C (350F/Gas 4). Mash the parsnips with half the butter, the cream, nutmeg and egg. Season with pepper, and salt if necessary. Turn the mixture into a buttered ovenproof dish. Melt the remaining butter and pour over the top.
3 Sprinkle with breadcrumbs and bake for 20-25 minutes until puffed up and golden brown. Serve hot, with roasts and casseroles. *Serves 4-6.*

Celery with Bay & Bacon

Celery is an under-rated vegetable, particularly as a hot accompaniment. The strong taste of the raw vegetable is muted and softened by cooking. I like to serve this dish with beef or game.

1 head celery
salt and pepper to taste
30g (1oz) butter
1 small onion, chopped
2 rashers back bacon, chopped
2 bay leaves

1 Cut the celery into 7.5cm (3 inch) lengths, then into broad strips. Cook in boiling salted water to cover for 10 minutes, Drain, reserving 3 tablespoons of the cooking liquid.
2 Heat the butter in a saucepan, add the onion and cook for about 5 minutes until softened. Add the bacon and cook for a further 5 minutes, until the bacon is slightly crispy. Add the celery, bay leaves, salt and pepper, and the reserved cooking liquid.
3 Bring to the boil, cover and cook gently for 20 minutes, until the celery is tender. Serve hot. *Serves 4-6.*

FENNEL WITH BAY AND BACON: Replace the celery with 3 fennel bulbs, cored and sliced. Serve as a delicious accompaniment to chicken dishes.

Carrot & Celeriac Bake

A purée of carrot and celeriac is the perfect accompaniment to a host of warming winter dishes. The addition of eggs and grated cheese makes it substantial enough to serve as a meal in itself, if you prefer.

500g (1lb) carrots
500g (1lb) celeriac
30g (1oz) butter
salt and pepper to taste
2 teaspoons chopped thyme (optional)
freshly grated nutmeg
3 eggs, beaten
90g (3oz) gruyère cheese, grated
1 tablespoon fresh breadcrumbs
TO GARNISH:
parsley or thyme sprigs

1 Peel the carrots and celeriac and cut them into even-sized chunks. Cook in boiling salted water for 15-20 minutes, until tender.
2 Preheat the oven to 180C (350F/Gas 4). Drain and mash the vegetables together, or purée them in a blender or food processor. Add the butter, salt, pepper, thyme if using, and nutmeg; mix well. Stir in the beaten eggs and 60g (2oz/½ cup) of the cheese.
3 Turn into a buttered ovenproof dish and sprinkle with the breadcrumbs and remaining cheese. Bake in the oven for 35-40 minutes, until risen and golden brown. Serve hot, garnished with parsley or thyme. *Serves 4-6.*

VARIATION: Use swede or turnip in place of the celeriac.

Rosemary Roast Potatoes

If you prefer, you can cook these around the roast where they will absorb the flavoursome meat juices. Choose smallish even-sized potatoes if possible, to avoid having to cut them into chunks.

1kg (2lb) small old potatoes
4-5 sprigs rosemary
3 tablespoons olive oil
coarse sea salt and pepper to taste
rosemary sprigs to garnish

1 Preheat the oven to 200C (400F/Gas 6). Peel the potatoes and make deep cross cuts on each, almost cutting right through. Strip rosemary leaves from stalks and chop them.
2 Place the potatoes in a roasting tin and sprinkle with the rosemary, oil, salt and pepper. Turn the potatoes to coat thoroughly. Bake for 1-1¼ hours until golden brown and cooked through. Serve garnished with rosemary. *Serves 6-8.*

Grated Potato Cakes

Vegetarians can omit the bacon and add a little chopped spring onion (green shallot) instead.

750g (1½lb) potatoes
2 rashers streaky bacon
1 clove garlic (optional)
salt and pepper to taste
1 egg, beaten
2 tablespoons chopped parsley
olive oil for shallow frying
parsley sprigs to garnish

1 Scrub the potatoes and steam them in their skins or cook in boiling salted water until almost tender. Leave to cool, then peel off the skins and coarsely grate the potatoes.
2 Grill the bacon until crisp, then crumble into the potato. Add the garlic if using, salt, pepper, egg and parsley; mix well. Shape the mixture into small flat cakes.
3 Heat the oil in a frying pan and fry the potato cakes for 2-3 minutes each side, until crisp and golden brown. Drain on kitchen paper and serve garnished with parsley. *Serves 4-6.*

Potato Purée with Tahini

This Middle Eastern style treatment for mashed potato makes it really rich and full of flavour. It can be prepared up to the baking stage a few hours in advance.

750g (1½ lb) potatoes
salt and pepper to taste
125ml (4 fl oz/½ cup) milk
3 tablespoons olive oil
1 onion, finely chopped
4 tablespoons tahini paste
2 teaspoons sesame seeds
½ teaspoon paprika
mint sprigs to garnish

1 Peel the potatoes, cut them into even-sized chunks and cook in boiling salted water until tender, about 25 minutes. Drain well and mash them with the milk and pepper.
2 Preheat the oven to 190C (375F/Gas 5). Heat the oil in a small pan, add the onion and fry for about 5 minutes, until softened and lightly browned. Add half of the onion to the potatoes with the tahini paste. Mix well.
3 Put the potato mixture into an oiled ovenproof dish and spread evenly. Add the sesame seeds to the remaining onion in the pan and cook for about 2 minutes, until the seeds are lightly browned. Scatter over the top of the potato and sprinkle with paprika.
4 Bake in the preheated oven for 20-25 minutes, until the topping is golden brown. Serve hot, garnished with mint sprigs. *Serves 4-6.*

NOTE: Tahini paste is a sesame seed paste widely used in the Middle East. It is available from delicatessens and larger supermarkets.

ARTICHOKE PUREE WITH TAHINI: Replace the potatoes with Jerusalem artichokes.

Carrots & Celery with Chilli

The warm flavour of chilli really enhances this vegetable mixture. Add more chilli sauce if you prefer it hot.

500g (1lb) carrots
4 celery sticks
1 small onion
½ red pepper
2 teaspoons olive oil
2 teaspoons chilli sauce
salt to taste
shredded spring onion (green shallot) to garnish

1 Peel the carrots. Cut the carrots and celery into even-sized sticks. Dice the onion and pepper. Heat the oil in a saucepan, add the onion and fry until softened, about 5 minutes. Add the carrots and celery and stir well. Cover and cook gently for about 10 minutes until the vegetables are almost tender, but with a firm bite.
2 Stir in the red pepper, chilli sauce and salt. Cover and cook for a further 5 minutes. Serve immediately, sprinkled with spring onion (shallot). *Serves 4-6.*

Baby Corn with Prosciutto

Use cheaper end cuts of prosciutto (or Parma ham) for this dish. The combination of sweet corn cobs and cured ham is very good.

1 tablespoon olive oil
30g (1oz) butter
30g (1oz) prosciutto, roughly chopped
250g (8oz) baby corn cobs
salt and pepper to taste

1 Melt the oil and butter in a small saucepan, add the prosciutto and fry until it starts to become crispy.
2 Stir in the corn cobs, salt and pepper. Add 1 tablespoon water, cover and cook for about 5 minutes, until the corn is tender. Serve hot. *Serves 4.*

Braised Aubergines (Eggplants)

Serve these hot or cold as an accompaniment, salad or starter.

500g (1lb) aubergines (eggplants)
salt and pepper to taste
3 tablespoons olive oil
1 clove garlic, crushed
1 teaspoon chopped oregano or ½ teaspoon dried
1 teaspoon paprika

1 Cut the aubergines (eggplants) into 2.5cm (1 inch) chunks and place in a colander. Sprinkle with salt and leave to drain for 30 minutes. Rinse and pat dry with kitchen paper.
2 Heat the oil in a saucepan, add the aubergines (eggplants) and fry for about 5 minutes, stirring all the time. Add the garlic and cook for 1 minute. Stir in the oregano, paprika, salt and pepper. Lower the heat, cover and cook for 15-20 minutes, until the aubergines (eggplants) are tender but not mushy. Serve hot or cold. *Serves 4.*

Sweet & Sour Mushrooms

2 tablespoons sunflower oil
1 small onion, chopped
1 stick celery, chopped
500g (1lb) cup mushrooms, sliced
1 tablespoon Worcestershire sauce
125ml (4 fl oz/½ cup) red wine
2 teaspoons French mustard
2 tablespoons soft brown sugar
salt and pepper to taste
shredded spring onion (green shallot) to garnish

1 Heat the oil in a saucepan, add the onion and celery and fry until softened, about 5 minutes.
2 Add the mushrooms and stir well. Add the remaining ingredients and bring to the boil, stirring all the time. Simmer, uncovered, for 15-20 minutes, until the mushrooms are tender and the sauce is slightly thickened.
3 Serve hot, garnished with spring onion (shallot), as a starter or accompaniment to grills and barbecues. *Serves 4-6.*

Crispy Baked Onions

Both red and white onions can be used for this tasty dish, which can be served hot or cold. If serving cold, choose red onions for their sweet taste. They make a good starter, either served on their own on a bed of salad leaves, or with other dishes. Hot crispy baked onions go well with grills and barbecues.

4 medium-sized onions
60g (2oz) butter
salt and pepper to taste
45g (1½oz/⅔ cup) fresh breadcrumbs
2 tablespoons grated Parmesan cheese
2 teaspoons chopped thyme, or 1 teaspoon dried

1 Preheat the oven to 190C (375F/Gas 5). Peel the onions and cut them in half crossways. Place in a buttered dish and dot the tops with half of the butter. Season with salt and pepper and cover with foil. Bake in the oven for about 1 hour, until the onions are almost tender.

2 Melt the remaining butter and mix with the breadcrumbs, cheese, thyme, salt and pepper. Uncover the onions and spread each one with a little of the breadcrumb mixture. Return to the oven and cook uncovered for 15-20 minutes, until the topping is crisp and golden brown. Serve hot. *Serves 4-8.*

CRISPY BAKED LEEKS: Use 750g (1½lb) leeks, cut into 10cm (4 inch) lengths, instead of the onions. Reduce the initial cooking time to 35-40 minutes.

Broccoli with Sesame Seeds

500g (1lb) broccoli
1 tablespoon oil
salt to taste
1 tablespoon sesame seeds
1 clove garlic, chopped
1 tablespoon soy sauce

1 Cut the broccoli into florets. Peel the stalks if thick, and cut diagonally into thin slices. Parboil the broccoli in boiling salted water for 3-4 minutes, then drain and cool quickly under running cold water.

2 Heat the oil in a frying pan or wok. Add the sesame seeds and garlic and stir-fry until golden brown. Add the broccoli and stir well. Add the soy sauce and cook, stirring for 2-3 minutes. Serve hot or cold. *Serves 4.*

Broccoli & Orange Butter Sauce

This is particularly good with cape broccoli and romanesco cauliflower – as they both have a tender melting texture.

500g (1lb) broccoli
ORANGE BUTTER SAUCE:
4 tablespoons fresh orange juice
1 tablespoon tarragon vinegar
salt and pepper to taste
125g (4oz) unsalted butter
2-3 tablespoons hot vegetable stock
TO GARNISH:
orange rind shreds

1 Cut the broccoli into florets and steam or cook in boiling salted water until just tender, about 7-10 minutes; drain.

2 Meanwhile make the sauce. Place the orange juice, vinegar, salt and pepper in a small pan. Bring to the boil and boil rapidly until reduced to 1 tablespoon.

3 Remove from the heat and whisk in the butter, a piece at a time, until a smooth creamy sauce is formed. If the sauce becomes too thick, whisk very briefly over the heat.

4 Gradually whisk in enough stock to yield a pouring consistency. Pour the sauce over the broccoli and garnish with orange shreds. *Serves 4.*

Potato Skins with Garlic Sauce

This makes a great starter, or you can serve it with other dishes as a casual lunch. If it is more convenient, the potatoes can be baked and scooped out ready for frying, and the sauce can be made several hours in advance.

6 large baking potatoes
oil for deep frying
SAUCE:
125ml (4 fl oz/½ cup) natural yogurt
1 clove garlic, crushed
2 tablespoons chopped mint
2 spring onions (green shallots), chopped
1 teaspoon paprika

1 Preheat the oven to 200C (400F/Gas 6). Scrub and dry the potatoes. Bake in the oven for 1-1¼ hours until tender. When cool enough to handle, halve the potatoes and scoop out the insides, leaving the skins with a 1cm (½ inch) thickness of potato flesh. (Use the scooped out potato for another dish.) Cut each potato half into 4-6 wedges.
2 Place all the sauce ingredients in a bowl and mix well. Transfer the sauce to a serving dish and chill until required.
3 Heat the oil in a deep-fryer to 180C (350F) or until a cube of day-old bread browns in 45 seconds. Fry the potato skins in the hot oil in batches for 3-4 minutes until they are golden brown and crisp. Drain well on kitchen paper and serve warm, with the sauce for dipping. *Serves 4.*

Pumpkin with Ginger & Orange

500g (1lb) pumpkin
2 tablespoons sunflower oil
1 teaspoon grated fresh root (green) ginger
2 tablespoons wine vinegar
1 tablespoon brown sugar
3 tablespoons orange juice
1 teaspoon grated orange rind
salt and pepper to taste
chopped parsley to garnish

1 Peel the pumpkin, discard the seeds and slice thinly. Heat the oil in a large pan, add the pumpkin and fry on both sides until golden. Add the ginger and stir well.
2 Add the remaining ingredients and simmer gently for about 10 minutes, stirring occasionally, until the pumpkin is tender. Serve hot, garnished with parsley. *Serves 4-6.*

Artichoke Hearts & Pistachios

juice of 2 lemons
4 large artichokes
salt and pepper to taste
30g (1oz) shelled pistachio nuts
60g (2oz) butter
1 tablespoon chopped parsley

1 Add the lemon juice to a bowl of water large enough to hold the artichoke hearts. Using a sharp knife, remove the top half of an artichoke. Strip off the tough outer leaves, then cut the artichoke into quarters. Working quickly, remove the hairy choke in each quarter and trim off any tough leaves. Place in the water with a saucer on top to keep it submerged. Prepare the other artichokes in the same way.
2 Transfer the artichokes and lemon water to a large saucepan and add salt. Bring to the boil, cover and simmer for 15-20 minutes, until the artichokes are tender; drain.
3 Meanwhile, place the pistachios in a small bowl and cover with boiling water. Leave for 5 minutes, then drain and slip off the skins. Chop the pistachios.
4 Melt the butter in a saucepan, add the artichokes and fry for 2-3 minutes. Add the nuts, pepper and parsley. Heat through and serve, as a starter or accompaniment. *Serves 4.*

Stir-fried Chinese Greens

Go into any Chinese supermarket and you will find a great selection of fresh greens, tied into neat bundles. Use pak choi, joy choi, Chinese leaves or chrysanthemum greens with small yellow flowers. Alternatively, try using Swiss chard, spring greens or spring cabbage.

500g (1lb) Chinese greens or Chinese leaves
2 tablespoons oil
1 dried red chilli
1 slice fresh root (green) ginger
1 tablespoon dry sherry
2 tablespoons soy sauce
4 tablespoons water
2 teaspoons sesame oil (optional)

1 Shred the greens. Heat the oil in a wok or frying pan with a lid. Add the chilli and ginger and stir-fry until the chilli darkens; remove it with a slotted spoon.
2 Add the greens and stir-fry until they begin to wilt. Mix together the sherry, soy sauce and water and add to the pan. Bring to the boil, cover and cook for 4-5 minutes, until the greens are tender. Stir in the sesame oil if using.
3 Serve immediately, as an accompaniment to oriental dishes or with a selection of other vegetable dishes. *Serves 4-6.*

VARIATION: For an extra hot flavour, sprinkle with 1-2 teaspoons shredded red chilli before serving.

Mushrooms in Vine Leaf Pie

Cooking mushrooms in a casing of vine leaves adds richness to their flavour and they look and smell wonderful when the leaves are peeled back.

12-16 fresh vine leaves
500g (1lb) open cup mushrooms
salt and pepper to taste
2 tablespoons olive oil
1 clove garlic, chopped
1 teaspoon coriander seeds, crushed
2 tablespoons lemon juice

1 Preheat the oven to 160C (325F/Gas 3). Use two thirds of the vine leaves to line an oiled 23cm (9 inch) pie dish or sandwich tin. Wipe the mushrooms clean and arrange in the dish, piling them up if necessary. Sprinkle with salt and pepper.
2 Heat the oil in a pan. Add the garlic and coriander seeds and fry for 2 minutes to bring out their flavours. Add the lemon juice, then pour the mixture evenly over the mushrooms. Cover with the remaining vine leaves, tucking in the ends neatly.
3 Cover the dish with foil and bake in the preheated oven for 35 minutes. Remove the foil and serve piping hot. *Serves 4-6.*

NOTE: If fresh vine leaves are not available, use a packet of preserved ones and soak them in boiling water for 15 minutes before use.

Chilli Sweet Potatoes

A Nigerian friend gave me this recipe. She claims it is the best way of cooking sweet potato – I hope you will agree! If you prefer a less hot flavour, omit the chilli seeds.

750g (1½ lb) sweet potatoes
1 tablespoon sunflower oil
1 onion, thinly sliced
1 red chilli, sliced into rings
salt to taste
parsley sprigs to garnish

1 Peel the sweet potatoes and cut into chunks. Heat the oil in a saucepan. Add the onion and fry for about 5 minutes, until softened and lightly browned. Add the chilli, together with its seeds, and fry, stirring, for 2 minutes.
2 Add the sweet potato and stir well. Add enough water to come halfway up the potato and bring to the boil. Add salt, cover and simmer for 10-15 minutes, until just tender.
3 Remove the lid and boil rapidly until almost all the liquid has evaporated. Serve hot, garnished with parsley. *Serves 4.*

Okra with Apricots

250g-375g (8-12oz) small okra
2 tablespoons orange juice
1 tablespoon olive oil
1 small onion, thinly sliced
125ml (4 fl oz/½ cup) passata
60g (2oz/½ cup) no-soak dried apricots, thinly sliced
salt and pepper to taste

1 Trim the okra stems, taking care not to cut into the pods. Place the okra in a bowl with the orange juice and mix well.
2 Heat the oil in a saucepan, add the onion and fry for about 5 minutes, until softened and lightly browned. Stir in the okra with the juice, cover and cook for 5 minutes.
3 Dilute the passata with an equal volume of water and add to the okra with the apricots, salt and pepper. Bring to the boil, then cook uncovered for 25-30 minutes, until the okra is tender and the sauce is thickened. Serve hot, with lamb, pork or other vegetables. *Serves 4-6.*

Summer Vegetable Stew

Use the sweetest, smallest early vegetables for this delightfully colourful dish. Serve it as a course by itself, with crusty bread to mop up the juices.

juice of 1 lemon
4 baby artichokes
2 ripe tomatoes
4 shallots
125g (4oz) baby carrots
500g (1lb) broad beans in pods
125g (4oz) French beans
250g (8oz) small new potatoes
2 tablespoons olive oil
125ml (4 fl oz/½ cup) dry white wine
125ml (4 fl oz/½ cup) vegetable stock or water
1 bouquet garni
salt and pepper to taste

1 Add the lemon juice to a bowl of water large enough to hold the artichokes. Trim the tops off the artichokes and remove any tough outside leaves. Cut the artichokes down through the heart into quarters and remove the chokes if they have formed. Place the artichokes in the lemon water with a saucer on top to keep them submerged.
2 Skin, seed and chop the tomatoes. Peel the shallots and cut each one into quarters, almost to the base. Scrape and trim the carrots, pod the broad beans, trim the French beans and scrub the potatoes.
3 Heat the oil in a saucepan, add the shallots and fry for 2-3 minutes, until lightly browned. Drain the artichokes and add to the pan, stirring well to coat in the oil. Add the wine, stock or water, bouquet garni, salt and pepper. Bring to the boil, cover the pan and simmer for 15 minutes.
4 Add the tomatoes, carrots, broad beans, French beans and potatoes. Bring back to the boil, then cook for a further 25-30 minutes, until all the vegetables are tender. Remove the bouquet garni before serving. *Serves 4-6.*

Courgette (Zucchini) Bake

This is an ideal dish to make when you are entertaining as it can be completely assembled well in advance. Make it in the summer when the tomatoes are full of flavour. Serve as a starter or accompaniment, or with crusty bread as a lunch or supper.

750g (1½lb) courgettes (zucchini)
500g (1lb) ripe tomatoes
4 tablespoons olive oil
2 onions, thinly sliced
2 teaspoons chopped thyme
salt and pepper to taste
1 tablespoon grated Parmesan cheese

1 Preheat the oven to 190C (375F/Gas 5). Top and tail the courgettes (zucchini), then cut into thin diagonal slices. Skin the tomatoes and cut into thin slices. Heat half the oil in a frying pan, add the onions and fry for 5-8 minutes, until they are soft and lightly browned.
2 Spread the onions over the base of a greased shallow ovenproof dish. Arrange alternate layers of courgettes (zucchini) and tomatoes over the onions, making sure each layer overlaps the previous one. Drizzle with the remaining oil and sprinkle with thyme, salt and pepper.
3 Bake in the preheated oven for 35-45 minutes. Sprinkle with Parmesan and bake for a further 10 minutes. Serve hot. *Serves 4-6.*

NOTE: To skin tomatoes, spear on a fork and hold over a gas flame for 15-30 seconds, turning until the skin blisters, then peel away the skins. Alternatively plunge into a bowl of boiling hot water and leave for 30 seconds, then peel.

VARIATION: For a more substantial supper dish, add 1 aubergine (eggplant) and 1 red pepper to the base; chop and fry with the onions.

Creamy Stuffed Tomatoes

The potato stuffing for these tomatoes is sweetened with a purée of yellow pepper and topped with melted gruyére cheese. Try serving as a light snack or to accompany casseroles or roasts.

8 medium-sized tomatoes
STUFFING:
500g (1lb) potatoes
salt and pepper to taste
1 yellow pepper
2 tablespoons oil
1 tablespoon chopped parsley
60g (2oz) gruyére cheese, grated
TO GARNISH:
salad leaves

1 Cut the tops off the tomatoes and scoop out the seeds and flesh. Leave them upside down in a colander to drain.
2 Peel the potatoes and cut into chunks. Cook in boiling salted water for about 20 minutes until tender, then drain and mash.
3 Preheat the oven to 190C (375F/Gas 5). Halve the pepper, remove the core and seeds and cut the flesh into small dice. Place in a small pan with the oil, salt and pepper. Cook gently for about 5 minutes, until the pepper is tender. Transfer to a blender or food processor and blend until smooth. Add to the potato with the chopped parsley and mix well. Taste and add more seasoning if necessary.
4 Place the tomatoes in an oiled ovenproof dish and carefully fill with the potato mixture. Sprinkle with the cheese and bake in the preheated oven for 15-20 minutes until the tomato is cooked and the topping is golden brown. Serve piping hot, garnished with salad leaves. *Serves 4 or 8.*

VARIATION: Use carrots or celeriac in place of the potatoes. Cook in salted water until tender, then drain and purée in a blender or food processor before adding the other ingredients.

Stuffed Vegetables

These stuffed vegetables are good served warm or cold as a starter, or as a main course with other dishes. They also reheat well.

125ml (4 fl oz/½ cup) virgin olive oil
4 spring onions (green shallots), chopped
185g (6oz/1¼ cups) long grain rice
125g (4oz/1 cup) dried apricots, chopped
small bunch of parsley, chopped
¼ teaspoon ground allspice
¼ teaspoon cayenne pepper
salt and pepper to taste
250ml (8 fl oz/1 cup) water
4 tomatoes
1 red pepper
1 green pepper
2 small aubergines (eggplants)
2 courgettes (zucchini)
2 tablespoons tomato purée (paste)

1 Preheat the oven to 180C (350F/Gas 4). Heat the oil in a saucepan, add the spring onions (shallots) and fry for 1 minute. Add the rice and stir well to coat. Add the apricots, parsley, allspice, cayenne, salt, pepper and water. Bring to the boil, then lower the heat, partially cover and cook for 10 minutes, until the rice is almost tender.
2 Remove the tops from the tomatoes and scoop out the seeds. Halve and seed the peppers. Halve the aubergines (eggplants) and courgettes (zucchini) lengthwise and scoop out some of the flesh. (Use the scooped out flesh for another dish.)
3 Place the vegetables in a buttered ovenproof dish or roasting tin and carefully fill them with the rice stuffing. Dilute the tomato purée (paste) with 500ml (16fl oz/2 cups) hot water and pour over the vegetables. Bake, uncovered, in the preheated oven for 45-55 minutes, until the vegetables are tender. *Serves 4.*

Stir-Fry with Gremolata

Gremolata is a combination of chopped parsley, garlic and lemon. Usually it is sprinkled over veal dishes, but I find it's delicious sprinkled over a selection of crunchy vegetables.

250g (8oz) broccoli
250g (8oz) cauliflower
2 medium-sized leeks
125g (4oz) mange tout (snow peas)
2 carrots, peeled
2 tablespoons sunflower oil
salt and pepper to taste
GREMOLATA:
1 teaspoon grated lemon rind
1 clove garlic, finely chopped
3 tablespoons chopped parsley

1 Cut the broccoli and cauliflower into small florets. Thinly slice the leeks. Top and tail the mange tout (snow peas). Using a potato peeler, pare the carrots into thin ribbons.
2 To make the gremolata, place the lemon rind, garlic and parsley in a small bowl and mix well.
3 Heat the oil in a frying pan with a lid, or a wok. Add the leeks, broccoli and cauliflower and stir-fry for 1 minute until the leeks start to soften. Add the carrot strips and stir-fry for a futher 1 minute.
4 Add 2 tablespoons water, cover and cook for 4 minutes, until the vegetables are just tender. Add the mange tout (snow peas), salt and pepper. Stir well, cover and cook for 1 minute.
5 Turn into a warmed serving dish and sprinkle with the gremolata. Serve immediately, with crusty bread as a light meal, or with other dishes. *Serves 4-6.*

Steamed Vegetables with Aioli

The cooking times for these vegetables are all important. They should retain all their crispness but lose their raw taste. The aioli can be made several days in advance and kept chilled until needed; leave at room temperature for an hour or so before serving.

500-750g (1-1½lb) assorted vegetables in season, ie broccoli, cauliflower, French beans, asparagus, carrots, courgettes (zucchini), mange tout (snow peas)
AIOLI:
2 egg yolks
1 teaspoon Dijon mustard
1 clove garlic, crushed
salt and pepper to taste
60ml (2 fl oz/¼ cup) olive oil
60ml (2 fl oz/¼ cup) sunflower oil
1 tablespoon lemon juice

1 First prepare the aioli. Place the egg yolks in a bowl with the mustard, garlic, salt and pepper. Beat lightly, then add the oils, a little at a time, beating constantly to form a thick sauce. Alternatively, prepare in a blender or food processor, adding the oils gradually through the feeder tube.
2 Stir in the lemon juice, and a little hot water if the aioli is too thick. Taste and add more seasoning if necessary. Transfer to a small serving dish.
3 Prepare all the vegetables. Break the broccoli and cauliflower into florets. Top and tail the French beans. Trim the asparagus spears. Scrub and trim the carrots, cutting them into sticks if large. Cut the courgettes (zucchini) into sticks. Top and tail the mange tout (snow peas).
4 Prepare a steamer or suspend a steaming basket over a saucepan of boiling water. Add the broccoli, cauliflower, French beans, asparagus and carrots to the steamer and cook for 3-4 minutes. Add the courgettes (zucchini) and steam for 2 minutes, then add the mange tout (snow peas) and steam for 1 minute.
5 If serving warm, arrange the vegetables on a serving platter with the aioli. If serving cold, first quickly refresh under cold water; drain well. Serve as a starter or light lunch. *Serves 4.*

Marinated Stuffed Peppers

These peppers are stuffed with scooped-out tomatoes which are in turn stuffed with mushrooms. Served warm or cold, they make a great starter.

4 green or yellow peppers (or 2 of each)
4 medium-sized tomatoes
90g (3oz) tiny button mushrooms
MARINADE:
2 cloves garlic, crushed
1 tablespoon chopped marjoram
60ml (2 fl oz/¼ cup) white wine
185ml (6 fl oz/¾ cup) olive oil
1 tablespoon lemon juice
1 teaspoon Dijon mustard
salt and pepper to taste
TO GARNISH:
marjoram sprigs

1 Remove the stalks from the peppers, then cut each pepper crossways in half. Scoop out the seeds and any white pith. Cut the tomatoes in half across the middle and scoop out the seeds and flesh. Sprinkle lightly with salt and leave upside down on a tray to drain. Cut any larger mushrooms into halves or quarters.
2 Place all the marinade ingredients in a bowl and whisk together until well blended.
3 Fit a tomato half inside each pepper half, then fill the centre of the tomato with mushrooms. Place the stuffed peppers in a shallow ovenproof dish and pour over the marinade as evenly as possible. Leave to marinate for about 1 hour.
4 Preheat the oven to 200C (400F/Gas 6). Bake the stuffed peppers for 30 minutes, until all the vegetables are tender, basting with the marinade halfway through cooking. Serve hot or cold, garnished with marjoram sprigs. *Serves 4-8.*

NOTE: These stuffed peppers can be cooked on the barbecue if they are wrapped in foil.

Spinach Stuffed Potatoes

I use medium-sized potatoes for this recipe as they cook more quickly, and look attractive. When spinach is out of season you can substitute 125g (4oz) frozen spinach.

6 potatoes, about 185g (6oz) each
250g (8oz) spinach
30g (1oz) butter
2 shallots, peeled and chopped
¼ teaspoon allspice
salt and pepper to taste
2 tablespoons grated Parmesan cheese

1 Preheat the oven to 200C (400F/Gas 6). Scrub the potatoes and pat dry with kitchen paper. Bake in the oven for about 45 minutes, until tender. When cool enough to handle, cut the potatoes in half and scoop out the flesh into a bowl. Mash thoroughly.
2 Wash the spinach in several changes of water; drain well. Melt the butter in a saucepan, add the shallots and cook for about 5 minutes until softened. Add the spinach and cook until just wilted, then cover and cook for 5 minutes, until tender. Add the potato, allspice, salt and pepper and mix well.
3 Place the potato shells in an ovenproof dish. Fill with the spinach mixture and sprinkle with cheese. Return to the oven for 20 minutes, until the topping is golden brown. Serve hot, as a snack or accompaniment to hot or cold dishes. *Serves 6.*

VARIATION: Replace the spinach with 2-3 tomatoes, skinned and finely chopped. *(Illustrated above right).*

Coriander Spiced Vegetables

Serve this lightly spiced curry with naan or pitta bread, or with rice and other curry dishes.

2 onions
3 cloves garlic
2 red or green chillies
2.5cm (1 inch) piece fresh root (green) ginger
1kg (2lb) mixed vegetables, ie potatoes, cauliflower, green beans, carrots
1 tablespoon coriander seeds
2 teaspoons cumin seeds
1 bay leaf
2 tablespoons oil
250g (8oz) can chopped tomatoes
250ml (8 fl oz/1 cup) water
salt and pepper to taste
125g (4oz) frozen peas
2 tablespoons chopped coriander leaves
coriander sprigs to garnish

1 Slice the onions thinly. Finely chop the garlic. Halve, seed and finely chop the chillies. Peel and finely chop the ginger. Peel the potatoes. Trim the rest of the vegetables and cut into even-sized chunks.
2 Crush the coriander and cumin seeds in a clean coffee grinder, or using a pestle and mortar. Break the bay leaf into several pieces.
3 Heat the oil in a large saucepan, add the onion and fry for about 5 minutes, until softened and lightly coloured. Add the garlic, chillies, ginger and bay leaf and fry for 2-3 minutes, stirring all the time. Add the ground spices and mix well. Add all the vegetables, except the cauliflower and peas, stirring them around to coat with the spices.
4 Add the tomatoes, water, salt and pepper. Bring to the boil, cover and simmer for 10 minutes, then add the cauliflower, peas and coriander leaves. Cook for a further 15-20 minutes, until the vegetables are tender. Serve garnished with coriander sprigs. *Serves 4-6.*

Fritters with Walnut Sauce

The dipping sauce for these light vegetables fritters is a more gutsy version of pesto. The vegetables I have used are suggestions only.

WALNUT SAUCE:
2 cloves garlic, crushed
12 basil sprigs
4 walnut halves
5 tablespoons olive oil
salt and pepper to taste
FRITTERS:
125g (4oz/1 cup) self-raising flour
1 teaspoon salt
250ml (8fl oz/1 cup) water
½ cauliflower
250g (8oz) courgettes (zucchini)
1 red pepper
oil for deep frying
TO GARNISH:
basil sprigs

1 To make the walnut sauce, grind the garlic, basil and walnuts using a pestle and mortar or clean coffee grinder until smooth. Gradually work in the olive oil to form a thick sauce. Season with salt and pepper.

2 To make the fritters, sift the flour and salt into a bowl. Gradually add the water, beating all the time, to form a smooth batter. Cut the cauliflower into florets, the courgettes (zucchini) into thick slices and the red pepper into broad strips. Add to the batter and stir carefully until all the vegetables are well coated.

3 Heat the oil to 180C (350F), or until a little batter added to the pan rises to the surface instantly, surrounded by bubbles. Fry the vegetables in batches in the hot oil for 2-3 minutes, until the batter is golden brown and crisp. Drain on absorbent kitchen paper and keep warm while frying the remaining vegetables.

4 Serve the vegetables on a warm serving platter with the bowl of walnut sauce, or arrange on individual serving plates with a spoonful of sauce. Garnish with basil. *Serves 4.*

Index